FAST CARS

ford
MUSTANG

by Lisa Bullard

Reading Consultant:
Barbara J. Fox
Reading Specialist
North Carolina State University

Content Consultant:
James Elliott
Editor
Classic & Sports Car magazine

Capstone
press

Mankato, Minnesota

Blazers is published by Capstone Press,
151 Good Counsel Drive, P.O. Box 669, Mankato, Minnesota 56002.
www.capstonepress.com

Library of Congress Cataloging-in-Publication Data
Bullard, Lisa.
Ford Mustang / by Lisa Bullard.
    p. cm.—(Blazers. Fast cars)
    Includes bibliographical references and index.
    ISBN-13: 978-1-4296-0100-9 (hardcover)
    ISBN-10: 1-4296-0100-0 (hardcover)
    1. Mustang automobile—Juvenile literature. I. Title. II. Series.
TL215.M8B85 2008
629.222'2—dc22   2007005675

Summary: Briefly describes the history and models of the Ford Mustang.

Editorial Credits
Erika L. Shores, editor; Bobbi J. Wyss, designer; Jo Miller, photo researcher

Photo Credits
Alamy/Motoring Picture Library, 6; Transtock Inc./Guy Spangenberg, 24–25
Corbis/Bettmann, 7; Car Culture, 14 (top)
Photo by Ted Carlson/Fotodynamics, 4–5, 20–21
Ron Kimball Stock/Ron Kimball, cover, 8–9, 12 (bottom), 13 (both),
    16–17, 22–23, 26–27, 28–29
Shutterstock/Joseph Aaron, 10–11, 12 (top); Lee Morris, 14 (bottom)
ZUMA Press/Harvey Swartz, 18–19

Essential content terms are **bold** and are defined at the
bottom of the page where they first appear.

1 2 3 4 5 6 12 11 10 09 08 07

TABLE OF CONTENTS

THE PONY CAR

A Ford Mustang burns rubber. Everyone stares as the cool car races down the street. Mustangs have been in the spotlight for years.

Early Mustangs were so popular that they started a **trend**. Other carmakers wanted to copy Ford's success. They built their own small, sporty cars. These cars became known as pony cars.

trend — a new design or the direction in which things are changing

1967 Chevrolet Camaro

1966 Ford Mustang convertible

fast fact

The first Mustangs had an ornament of a running horse in the front grille.

chapter 2

FORTY FABULOUS YEARS

The first Mustangs hit the streets in April 1964. The car looked fast and fun. Many young drivers could afford to buy the inexpensive Mustang.

Drivers soon wanted faster Mustangs with better **performance**. Ford added bigger engines to Mustang models like the 1969 Mach 1. The Mach 1 is famous for its shaker scoop on the front hood.

performance — describes a car's power, handling, and ability to achieve speed

shaker scoop

fast fact

The scoop on the Mach 1's hood shook when the engine idled.

MUSTANG TIMELINE

Mustang Mach I is introduced.

1969

1964

1974

The smaller Mustang II takes over.

Ford Mustang is introduced.

Mustang models changed through the years. The Fox-body style appeared in 1979. It replaced the smaller Mustang II.

Shelby Cobra GT500 is released.

2007

1979

1994

Ford's Mustang redesign is called the Fox-4 or SN-95.

Mustang Fox-body is introduced.

1968 Ford Mustang 428 Cobra Jet

2005 Ford Mustang

Ford gave Mustang a new design in 2005. The new Mustang shares styling features with early Mustangs. These include the sharklike nose and fastback roofline.

fast fact

A new design in 1994 brought back Mustang's galloping pony symbol to the front grille.

chapter 3

SHELBY MUSTANGS

Mustangs weren't speed kings until Shelby Mustangs came along. Former race car driver Carroll Shelby designed these Mustangs from 1965 to 1970.

1967 Shelby Mustang GT500

Today, Ford is working with Shelby again. The 2007 Ford Shelby Cobra GT500 is the most powerful production Mustang ever built. Its supercharged V8 engine produces 500 **horsepower**.

horsepower — a unit for measuring an engine's power

chapter 4

THE MUSTANG LOOK

deck

Mustangs are known for certain design features. One of the most famous features is the long front hood combined with a short rear **deck**.

deck — the area of a car between the cockpit and the back bumper

hood

From behind, drivers notice another Mustang feature. They can see the Mustang's famous three-part taillights.

Ford has always offered buyers different models of the Mustang. One very popular choice is the **convertible** body style.

> **convertible** — a car with a top that can be lowered or removed

MUSTANG DIAGRAM

high-intensity headlamp

hood

grille

bumper

spoiler

deck

GT 500

alloy wheel

chapter 5

MUSTANG GALLOPS AHEAD

Ford plans to introduce a new Mustang design every year. Fans can't wait to see if a new Mustang can top the Mustangs of the past.

2007 Shelby Cobra GT500 (left) and
1966 Ford Shelby GT350 (right)

GLOSSARY

convertible (kuhn-VUR-tuh-buhl)—a car with a top that can be lowered or removed

deck (DEK)—the area of a car between the cockpit and the back bumper

grille (GRIL)—an opening, usually covered by grillwork, for allowing air to cool the engine of a car

horsepower (HORSS-pou-ur)—a unit for measuring an engine's power

model (MOD-uhl)—the new design of a car that comes out each year

performance (pur-FOR-muhnss)—describes a car's power, handling, and ability to achieve speed

production (pruh-DUHK-shuhn)—describes a vehicle produced for mass-market sale

trend (TREND)—a new design or the direction in which things are changing

READ MORE

Hawley, Rebecca. *Mustang.* Superfast Cars.
New York: Rosen, 2007.

Kimber, David. *Auto-Mania.* Vehicle-Mania!
Milwaukee, Gareth-Stevens, 2004.

Maurer, Tracy Nelson. *Muscle Cars.* Roaring
Rides. Vero Beach, Fla.: Rourke, 2004.

INTERNET SITES

FactHound offers a safe, fun way
to find Internet sites related
to this book. All of the sites
on FactHound have been
researched by our staff.

Here's how:
1. Visit *www.facthound.com*
2. Choose your grade level.
3. Type in this book ID **1429601000** for
   age-appropriate sites. You may also
   browse subjects by clicking on letters,
   or by clicking on pictures and words.
4. Click on the **Fetch It** button.

FactHound will fetch the best sites for you!

INDEX